Teach Yourself Stitch Craft and Dressmaking

Volume IV: Pattern Drafting for Men and Practice Drafts

Trying your hand at drafting shirts

I0435476

Dueep Jyot Singh

Learning Series

Mendon Cottage Books

JD-Biz Publishing

Download Free Books!

http://MendonCottageBooks.com

Our books are available at

1. Amazon.com
2. Barnes and Noble
3. Itunes
4. Kobo
5. Smashwords
6. Google Play Books

Download Free Books!

http://MendonCottageBooks.com

Table of Contents

Introduction

In my previous books of this series, I touched a little bit upon pattern drafting, and how you can make your own patterns with a little bit of know-how. But when you are doing the pattern drafting for men, the drafting is going to be different than what how you do it for women and children. That is, of course, natural, because the body build is different, and so are the measurements.

For example, the proportion of the depth of scye [i.e – the distance from the neck to the armpit] is going to change, according to the size of the chest. In tailoring, this is called a working scale. This working scale is a means of comparison from which we are able to compute the relative values of the depth and the width in their relation to the circumference of the chest. This is normally done in men as per the table given on the next page.

Number	Chest measurement	Working scale
1	Up to 71 cm – 28 inches	Half the chest, +1.5 cm [1/2 inches]
2	From 71 – 92 cm [28 – 36 inches]	Half the chest
3	From 92 cm [36 inches] and more	1/3 chest +15 cm [6 inches]

You can see from number 3 that the scale is going to give the essential decreasing ratio of depth qualities. These are necessary for large sizes. When the chest is more than 36 inches, the scye depth measurement [the distance of 0 – 1 in a draft when you are making a coat] is always going to be calculated as 1/6th of the chest measurement +7.5 cm or 3 inches. This proportion of scye depth is always half the working scale as given in the number 3 of the chest measurement. So instead of ¼, 1/6, 1/8, 1/12 of the chest proportions, you need to use ½, 1/3, ¼, or 1/6 of the scale proportions.

The values found from the scale are not going to be the exact values but nearer to it. For the exact values, people use direct measurement values. But that is going to differ from person to person.

Nevertheless, when we are talking about drafting men's garments like shirts and coats, the scye depth measurement is changed according to the chest.

For example, when we are drafting out Manila Shirts or short coats, 1 – 0 [the scye depth] is going to be equal to 1/4th of the chest. This proportion is going to suit well for a chest from 72 – 92 cm [28 – 36 inches.] But when the chest is more than 92 cm or 36 inches and above, the distance is going to be kept 1/6 chest +7.5 cm [3 inches] and for a chest, up to 28 cm, this distance is going to be equal to ¼ chest +1.25 cm [1/2 inches].

So when we are making patterns with large and small measures, whenever there is the proportion of 1/12th chest – if you see any pattern, where the neck width in a 2 button single breasted coat with a step collar, and with one breast pocket, and 2 double jetted cut pockets with flaps –, you are going to take it as 1/3 of the scye depth.

The sleeve width is also going to be adjusted according to the width of the scye depth.

For tighter fitting shirts, the proportion of the scye depth is going to be lessened by 1.25 cm or half an inch.

Taking Measurements

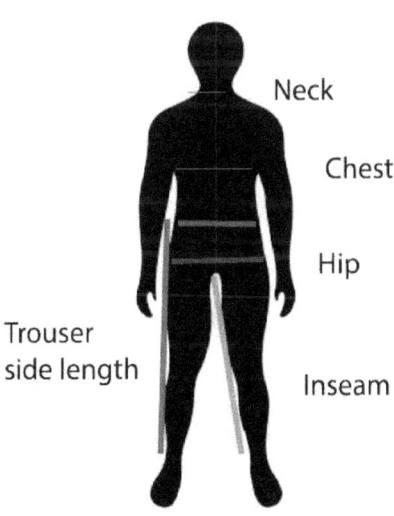

For men, these are the measurements normally taken. Also, the arm and sleeve measurements.

Normal measurements taken for both men and women.

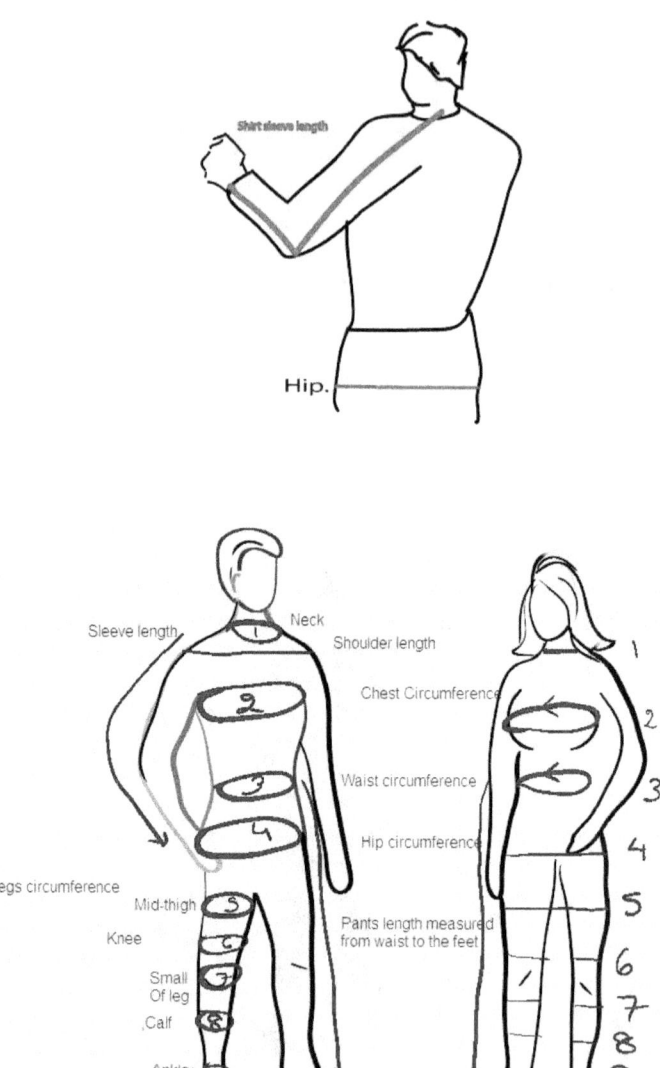

Shirt sleeve length

Hip.

Sleeve length
Neck
Shoulder length
Chest Circumference
Waist circumference
Hip circumference
Legs circumference
Mid-thigh
Knee
Pants length measured from waist to the feet
Small Of leg
Calf
Ankle

Introduction to Shirts

A shirt is a loose garment for the upper part of the body. This is prepared in many styles, and different fashions according to where you find yourself on the globe. The popular and common types, which you are going to learn to draft in this book are half and full open shirts with half and full sleeves and with open or closed collars. The next book is going to tell you all about how you can make sleeves and collars, according to the dictates of fashion and using your own creativity.

A shirt measurement is taken around the neck – measured around the base of the throat. After that you are going to do the chest measurement, measured around the fullest part of the chest just under the arms and straight across the back. The tape is going to be kept parallel to the floor.

The full length measurement is taken from the shoulder line close to the neck to the desired length of the garment. This length is going to differ in various garments. Always keep the tape straight down the front.

The waist length measurement is the measurement from the nape to the hollow of the waist line taken from the back.

The shoulder measurement is measured from the nape to the shoulder and at the sleeve joint.

The sleeve length is the length from the shoulder and to the desired length of the sleeve. This is also taken from the nape over the shoulder to the required length.

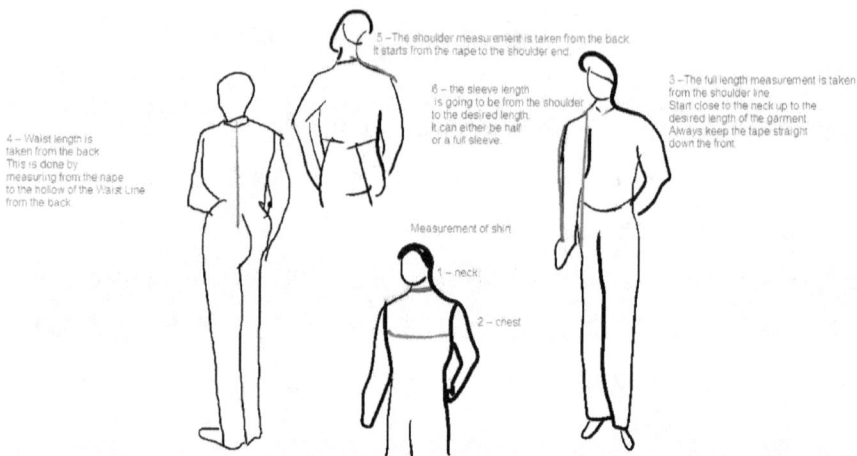

4 – Waist length is taken from the back. This is done by measuring from the nape to the hollow of the Waist Line from the back.

5 –The shoulder measurement is taken from the back. It starts from the nape to the shoulder end.

6 – the sleeve length is going to be from the shoulder to the desired length. It can either be half or a full sleeve.

3 –The full length measurement is taken from the shoulder line. Start close to the neck up to the desired length of the garment. Always keep the tape straight down the front.

Measurement of shirt

1 – neck

2 – chest

Half back measurement

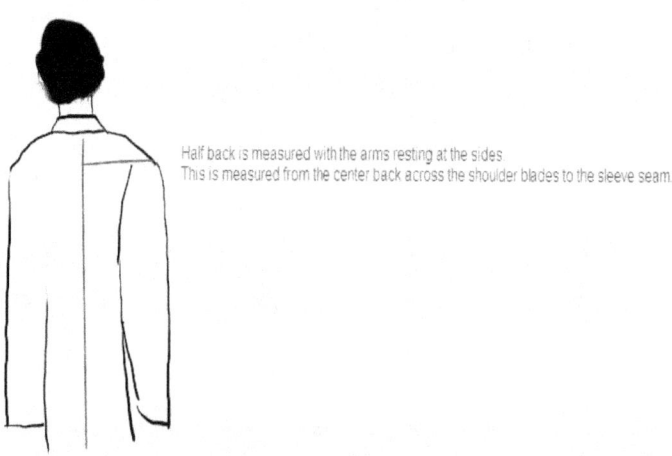

Half back is measured with the arms resting at the sides. This is measured from the center back across the shoulder blades to the sleeve seam.

How loose fitting the shirt is, is generally a matter of taste. For non stretchable material, you can do the loosing around the chest, which is kept generally 7.5 – 20 cm [3 – 8 inches.] If you want a more slender shape at the

---

waist, you can suppress the material at the sides near the waist line. When we are going to make a draft for a Manila shirt, we are going to take darts at the back. Also we are going to draft out Manila shirts and Bush shirts, later on in the book.

The shoulder is also called the yoke. Shirts are generally prepared with shoulders, but some prefer it without a yoke like as you see in a lounge jacket.

The width of the yoke is generally going to be 1/8 of the chest like you are going to see in the half open shirt. If you want more width, lessen the back length at the top, according to the increased length of the yoke.

For a practice session to show you how the drafting for a half open shirt is done, we are going to start with a half open shirt where the opening of the shirt is nearly up to the waist.

Drafting for Half Open Shirt/T-Shirt

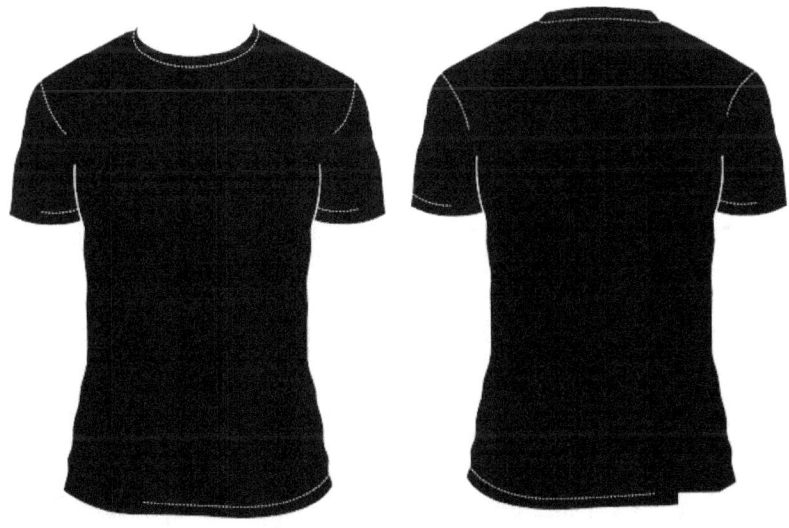

This is called a plain shirt with half sleeves, you can call it a half shirt and with full sleeves, it is going to become a full shirt. You can attach a collar according to the taste and fashion.

Material required

The material required for a half open full shirt with a 32 inch chest measurement is going to depend on the width of the cloth. If you are taking three fourth of the chest, plus about 3 inches, you are going to need 2 full lengths +2 sleeve lengths.

If the width of the cloth is nearly the same as the chest, you will need the full lengths plus one sleeve length +.25 m more.

If the width of the cloth is equal to chest +8 inches more, you will need 2 full lengths +.25 m more.

Measurements:

Neck – 35 cm [14"]

Chest – 80 cm [32"]

Full-length – 76 cm [30"]

Shoulder – 20 cm [8"]

Sleeves can be half and full.

Instructions for Drafting

Front Portion

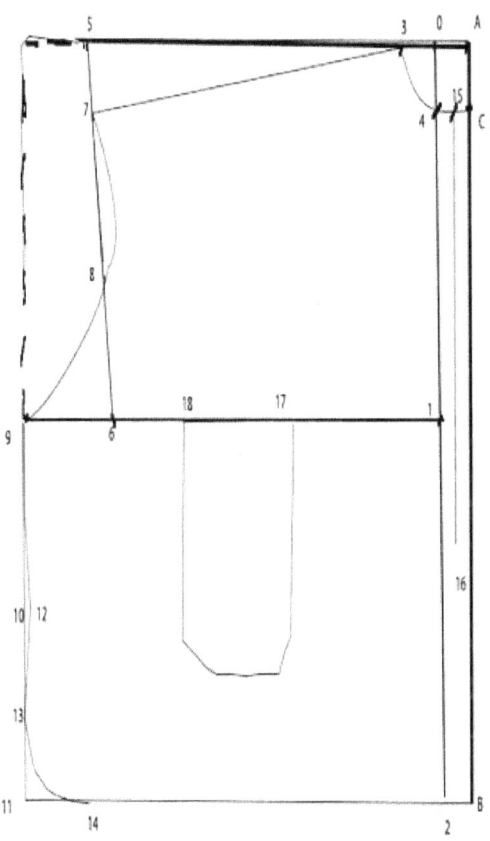

Make a fold with 2 points on it A – B [top and bottom of the fold.]

Line 0 – 1 – 2 is going to be at a distance of 4 cm [1 ½ inches] from the fold A – B.

1 – 0 is ¼ of the chest.

2 – 0 is full length, +2.5 cm [1"]

Square out from 0, 1 and 2. Squaring out means just extending the line horizontally or vertically, depending on what you are drafting.

3 – 0= 1/6 neck

4 – 0 = 1/6 neck +.75 cm [1/4"]

6 – 1= ¼ chest

5 – 0= shoulder +.75 cm [1/4"]

6 – 1= 1/4th chest.

Join 5 – 6

7 – 5= ¼ of 5 to 6

Join shoulder 3 – 7.

8 – 6= 3 cm [1 ¼"]

9 – 1= ¼ chest +5 cm [2"] or according to taste

Shape scye 7 – 8 – 9

Square down from 9 to 10 and 11.

10 – 9, is about 1/4th of the chest

12 – 10= 1.5 cm [1/2"]

13 is midway between 10 to 11

14 – 11= about 1/8 of the chest.

Shape 9 – 12 – 30 – 14 as you can see the draft.

15 – 4= 1.5 cm [1/2"]

16 – 15 is parallel to 1 – 0. This is equal to one fourth of the chest, +10 cm [4"]

Cut the lower layer from 15 – 16 of the right side. That means the left side should be wider than the right side. C – A is same as 3 – 0. Join 4 –C.

The pocket is going to be 17 – 1 and about 2 inches high. 18 – 17 equals to $1/8^{th}$ chest or +1.5 cm [half an inch width]. You can make it as deep as you want, or same as 18 to 17+1.5 cm [1/2 inches.]

Back draft

For making the back, you can cut the front and use it for the back in such a way that the lines 1 – 2 and 1 – 9 of the front and back coincide. You can also cut the back, in the following 2 instructions.

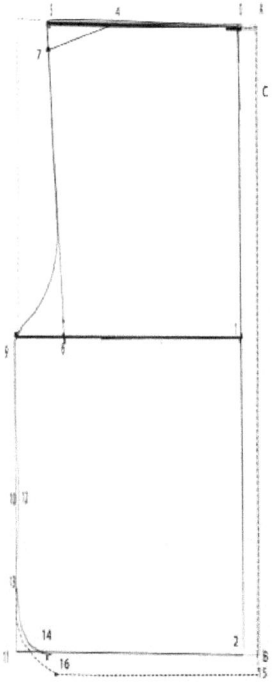

Ordinary Back

For drafting a plain back without any sort of pleats, or gathering – see above sketch, you are going to draft out the plan like this –

Square lines from 0, fold at 0 – 2.

1 – 0 is same as 1 – 0 of the front -4 cm [1 ½"].

2 – 1 is the same as 2 – 1 of the front.

Square out from 0, 1, and 2.

5 – 0= same as 5 – 0 of front.

Square down from 5 up to 6.

5 – 7= 1.5 cm [1/2"]

4 is midway between 5 – 0.

Shape 7-4, as I have done. You can do it according to your own choice.

Except for 8, the proportions of 9 – 1 are the same as those of the front.

Shape the scye carefully, which is 7 – 8 – 9.

Gathered or Pleated Back

Square lines from A, with the fold at A – B.

Draw the line 0 – 1 – 2 at a distance of 2 – 4 cm [3/4 to 1 ½"] from A – B.

The proportions of .1 – 14 are the same as you see in the back sketch, given above.

If you need a longer back, you are going to make the following changes. Increase the bottom by 2.5 – 4 cm [1 – 1 ½"] as you can see dotted out at C – 15 – 16 – 13.

There we are, we have finished the front and the back of the half open shirt.

Yoke – Shoulder

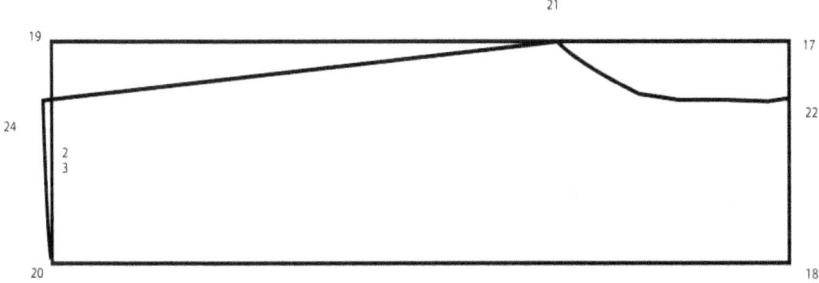

The neckline can be as deep as you wish, and so can the length of the sleeve.

For this, we are going to square lines from 17. The fold is at 17 – 18. 18 – 17 is 1/8 of the chest.

19 – 17= shoulder +.75 cm [1/4"]

20 – 18 is the same as 19 – 17. Join 20 – 19.

21 – 17= 1/6 the neck +.75 cm [1/4".]

22 – 17= this is the half of 21 – 17+1 cm [or 1/4"]

Shape the neck = 22 – 21

23 – 19= 3 cm [1 ¼ inches.] If you are designing for boys, keep it 2.5 cm or 1 inch.

Join 21 – 23 and add 0.75 cm to get .24. Join 24 and 20.

Full Open Shirt

Along with the drafting, you are going to learn how to stitch the shirt as practice.

Length – as per size.

Chest – circumference

Shoulder – width

Neck – circumference –

Full sleeve length.

We are drafting out a formal shirt.

0 – 1= measure full length, plus one inch and mark the point.

0 – A and 1 – B= measure and mark 1 ½ inches extension for a placket. The black. It is where you are going to place the buttons on the front of the shirt, and on the sleeves.

0 – 2= measure 1/4th of the chest, plus one and a half inches extra ease, plus half an inch seam for the width of the shirt and mark this point.

0 – 3= measure and mark same as 0 – 2. Draw a block 0 – 1 – 3 – 2

0 – 4= measure 1/4th of the chest for armhole length and mark this point.

0 – 5= measure half shoulder +1/4 inch and mark this point.

5 – 6= measure ¾ inch down for the shape of the shoulder and mark this point.

0 – 7= measure 1/12th just for front neck length and mark the point. Join 7 – 8.

4 – 9= measure the width of the shirt and mark this point.

5 – 6 – 10 is a straight line. Mark 11 as the center point of 5 – 10. Measure half an inch inside on 11 – 12 and mark this point. Use the French curve to draw the front armhole shape on 6 – 12 – 9.

13 is the center point of 7 – 8. Measure half an inch inside on 13 – 14 and draw a smooth V shape on 8 – 14 – 7.

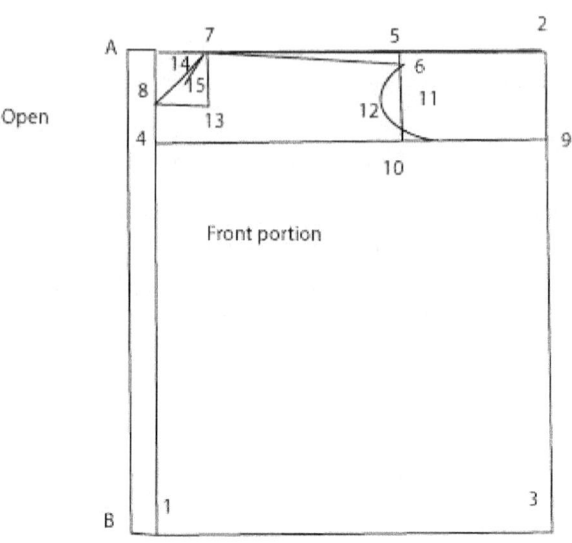

Back portion Draft

For the back portion, 0 – 1, 0 – 2, 1 – 3, 0 – 4, 0 – 5, 5 – 6, 0 – 7, 0 – 8, 4 – 9 and 5 – 6 – 10 points are going to be the same as they were on the front part.

11 – mark a Center point. On 5 – 10 draw back the armhole shape with the French curve on 11 – 9.

4 – 12 and 10 – 13= measure 1 ½ inches upwards and mark these points. Join 12 – 13 as a straight line.

13 – 14 – measure half an inch downwards and mark this point. Join 12 – 14.

Join 7 – 15 and 15 – 14 with the shape for a yoke of the shirt.

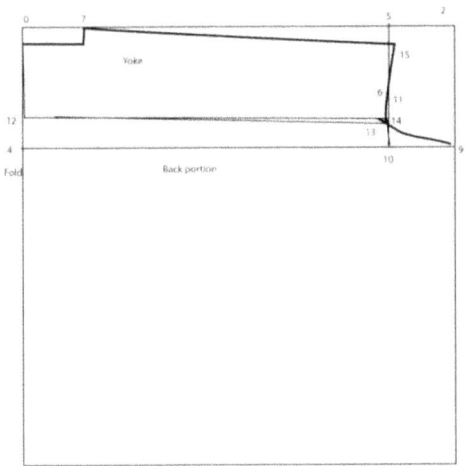

Pocket

0 – 1 and 2 – 3= measure 1/6 of the chest -1/4 inches +1 1/2 inches for fold as the length of the pocket, and mark that point.

0 – 2 and 1 – 3= measure 1/6 of the chest -1/4 inches for the width of the pocket, and mark that point.

0 – 4 and 2 – 5= 1 ½ inches for fold. Join 0 – 1 – 3 – 2 and 4 – 5.

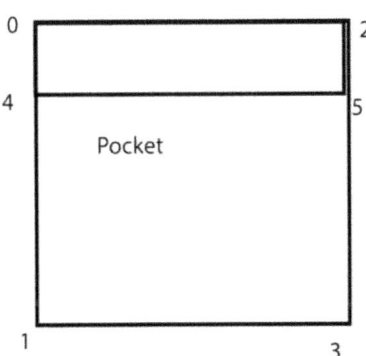

Sleeves

0 – 1= measure ½ chest, +4 inches for the length of the sleeve -2 ½ inches of the sleeve cuffs length. Mark this point.

0 – 2= measure ¼ chest for the width of the sleeve and mark that point.

1 – 3 is measured the same manner you did 0 – 2 and draw a rectangular block on 0 – 1 – 3 – 2.

4= mark a center point on 0 – 2.

5= mark a center point of 0 – 4.

2 – 6= measure and mark same as 2 – 4.

5 – 7= measure ¼ inches inwards and mark the point.

4 – 8= measure ½ inches inwards and mark the point.

8 – 9 = measure 1 ¼ inches inwards and mark the point.

3 – 10= measure 1 inch inwards and mark the point. Join 6 – 10.

Join 0 – 7 – 8 – 6 for back armhole shape. Join 7 – 9 – 6 for front armhole shape.

Mark 11 as the center point of 1 – 10. Measure 11 – 12 upwards , which is 1/6 of the chest for the open slit with the cuff.

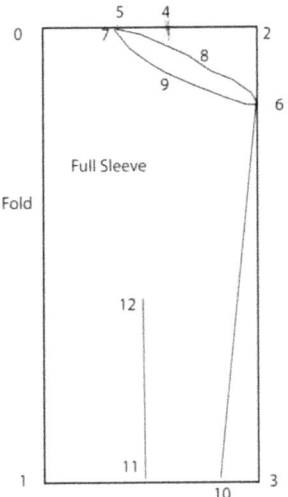

Sleeve cuff

0 – 1 and 2 – 3= measure 2 ½ inches length of the cuff and mark the point.

0 – 2 and 1 – 3= measure 1/8th of the chest, +2 ½ inches for the width of the cuff and mark the point.

2 – 5 and 2 – 4= measure half inches each and mark these points. Draw the curve shape on 4 – 5.

Sleeve Placket

0 – 1 and 2 – 3 =measure 5 inches plus cuff length and mark the point.

0 – 2 and 1 – 3= measure 1 width of 1 ½ inches and the other of 2 ½ inches.

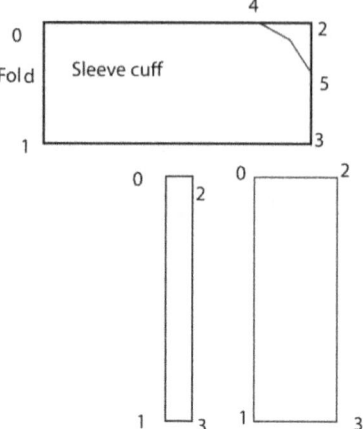

Sleeve cuff and sleeve placket.

Collar

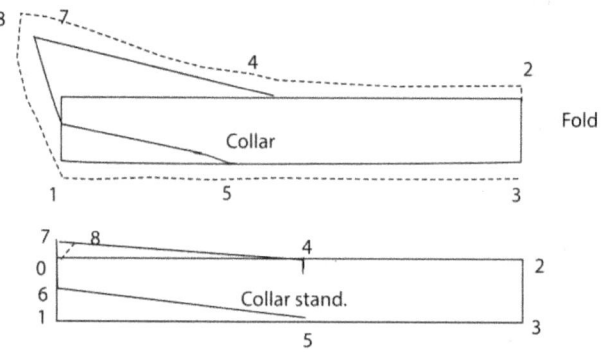

Collar and collar stand.

You are going to cut 2 front parts, one back portion, 2 pieces of the back yoke, 2 sleeves, 4 pieces of cuffs, 2 pieces narrow and 2 pieces wide sleeves plackets, 2 pieces of collar in the stand shape – and one piece of stiff buckram fabric as for the shape of the collar, and another piece of buckram as for the stand shape without any seam allowance.

1Strip of buckram of one and a half inches width is required for the front placket as per the length of the shirt and 2 pieces of buckram for the sleeve cuff, and 6 buttons for the buttonholes.

Stitching Instructions

Fold the placket part of the right hand side front and tack it with basting stitches.

Insert the buckram stitch inside the placket of the left-hand side part of the front and stitch 2 parallel seams.

Fold the pocket on 4 – 5 and stitch.

Place the pocket on the right-hand side part, 2 inches away from the placket and 1 ½ inches up from the armhole point.

Stitch this pocket.

Place the back portion in between the 2 pieces of the yoke and stitch on 1 – 3.

Turn and press the seam. Ironing after you have done some stitching is always necessary because that helps in setting the design properly.

Join the front and the back shoulder together. Place the buckram piece of the corner on the 2 pieces of the collar and joined them together.

Place the collar on the neck portion of the shirt and stitch together.

Join the sleeves placket.

Join 2 pieces of the cuff together on 0 – 2 – 3 by inserting the pieces of buckram.

Make 2 small pleats of half inch width on the wide placket side of the sleeves, and then baste by hand with needle.

Join the sleeves cuffs.

Mark a small notch on the center of the sleeves armhole and the shoulder of the shirt. Match together and join the sleeves on the 2 armhole sides of the shirt.

Join the 2 sides of the sleeve along with the short side seam on 10 – 9 and 7 – 8.

Fold the bottom of the shirt and stitch it. Stitch buttonholes on the front placket and buttons on the opposite side of the front part to finish up your shirt. Iron before wearing.

We are going to learn how to make collars and professional sleeves, later on in the series. This is just to show you how their draft looks like.

Now we come to the drafting of a Manila shirt. As far as the fashion requirements go, this shirt is prepared with either half or full sleeves and with an open or closed collar.

The top side of the back portion 0 – 8 is normally kept plain without any gathers and you can attach a plain shoulder yoke as I drafted one in the half open shirt. Some people prefer a curved yoke, extended to the center bottom. See the front shoulder yoke which I have given in the shirt draft down below? You can also attach that if you want.

Manila Shirt Draft

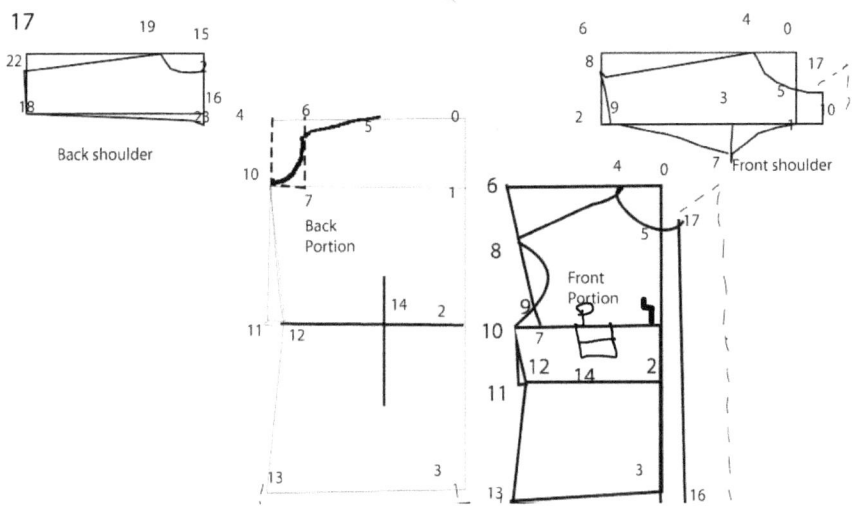

Measurements:

Neck – 35 cm [14"]

Chest – 80 cm [32"]

Full-length – 76 cm [30"]

Shoulder – 20 cm [8"]

Sleeves can be half and full.

Front Portion

You are going to take 2 layers of material and draft, as follows.

For an open collar, you are going to draw a line 0 – 1 – 3 from the edge – A – B at a distance of 7.5 – 9 cm [3 – 3 ½"] from the edge for facing. For example, this can be 6.25cm [2 ½ inches] for in turn +1.25 cm [half inch] and 1.25 cm [half"] for a button stand.

For a closed collar, you are going to draw the line 0 – 1 – 2 from the edge A – B at a distance of 5 cm [2 inches]. That will 3.75 cm [1 ½"] for inturns and 1.25 cm [half inch] for the button stand.

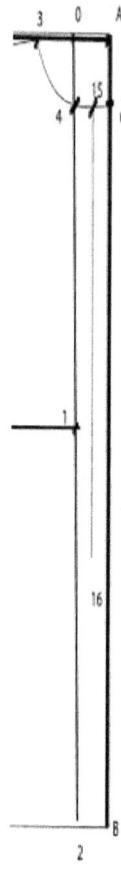

For the front portion start by squaring the lines from 0.

1 – 0 is ¼ of the chest -1.5 cm [1/2 inches.]

2 – 1= ¼ chest [or the waist length from 0.]

3 – 0 is the full length.

Square out from 1, 2 and 3.

4 – 0 is 1/6 of the neck.

5 – 0 is 16 of the neck +.75 cm [1/4"]. Shape the neck 5 – 4.

6 – 0 is the shoulder +.75 cm [1/4"]

7 – 1 is ¼ chest -1.5 cm [1/2"]. Join 6 and 7.

8 – 6 is ¼th of 6 to 7.

Join the shoulder 4 – 8.

9 – 7= about 3 cm [11/4"].

10 – 1 is ¼th of the chest, +5 cm – 2 inches – or according to your own taste.

Shape the arm scye 8 – 9 – 10.

11 is squared down from 10.

12 – 11 is half an inch – 1.5 cm.

13 – 3= 10 – 1+1.5 cm [half an inch.] The side seam is shaped as 10 – 12 – 13.

14 – 2= 1/12 of the chest, +1.5 cm [1/2 inches.] If required, you can take a small dart at 14.

15 – 3 is 2 centimeters. Shape the bottom portion 15 – 13.

16 – 15 and 17 – 5 are each 1.5 cm. Join 17 – 16.

The pockets are going to be drafted on the front portion on the 10 – 7 – 1 line.

For the Back Portion

You can either cut out the front and use it for the back in such a way that the lines 1 – 3 and 1 – 10 of the front and back coincide.

Square lines from 0, fold at 0 – 3. 1 – 0= 1 to 0 of the front -2.5 cm.

2 – 1 is same as 2 – 1 of the front.

3 – 1 is the same as 3 – 1 of the front.

Square out from. 1, 2 and 3.

6 – 0= shoulder +1 cm [1/4"]

5 is midway between 6 – 0.

Square down from 6 to 7.

8 – 6 is 1.5 cm or half an inch. Shape 0 – 5 – 8.

10 – 1 is same as the 10 – one of the front.

Shape the scye 8 – 9 – 10.

The proportions of 11 to 14 are going to be the same as that of the front.

Shape the side seam 10 – 12 – 13.

If required, you can take a dart at 14.

The back yoke – seen in the draft, as back shoulder – is prepared by extending the center bottom – .23 upwards. The proportions of points 15 – 22 are given in the half open shirt yoke draft. That means –

Yoke – Shoulder

For this, we are going to square lines from 17. The fold is at 17 – 18. 18 – 17 is 1/8 of the chest.

19 – 17= shoulder +.75 cm [1/4"]

20 – 18 is the same as 19 – 17. Join 20 – 19.

21 – 17= 1/6 the neck +.75 cm [1/4".]

22 – 17= this is the half of 21 – 17+1 cm [or 1/4"]

Shape the neck = 22 – 21

23 – 19= 3 cm [1 ¼ inches.] If you are designing for boys, keep it 2.5 cm or 1 inch.

Join 21 – 23 and add 0.75 cm to get .24. Join 24 and 20.

23 – 16= 4 – 6.5 cm [1 ½ – 2 ½ inches.]

You can shape 23 – 18, as seen in the draft given above, or if you want, you can have it as this shape. The shape is going to depend on how you would like the sleeve.

Each yoke is going to require 2 pieces – 23 – 18 – 22 – 19 – 20 – 23, which is the outer piece. And 16 – 18 – 22 – 19 – 20 – 16, which is the inner piece. The fold is going to be at 15 – 23.

Front yoke – if you want a front yoke, this is going to be drafted as follows.

1 – 5= 4 – 5 cm [1 ½ inches – 2"]

Square out to 1. 3 is midway between 2 to 1.

7 is squared down from 3 and is equal to 5 – 6 cm or 2 – 2 ½ inches.

Shape 9 – 7 and 1 – 7, as you can see in the draft, giving it the curve you want. The other proportions are going to be the same as the top side of the front.

Add a little bit of extra seam allowance at 9 – 7 – 1 – 10.

Safari Shirt

If you want something more challenging, we are going to draft out the Safari shirt which is normally made of tougher materials, like that from which we make pants and trousers. The back is normally kept plain or you can attach a belt at the back at 2 – 12.

You can also attach patch pockets. If you want to separate your from others, it is going to be attached at X – 19 and X – 17.

Measurements:

Neck – 35 cm [14"]

Chest – 80 cm [32"]

Full-length – 76 cm [30"]

Shoulder – 20 cm [8"]

Sleeves can be half and full.

Front Portion

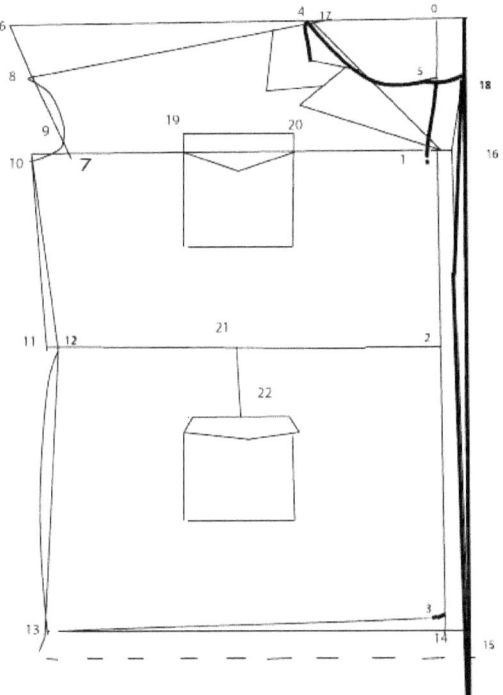

Draw a line 0 – 1 – 3 at a distance of nearly 4 cm [1 ½"] from the edge.

1 – 0 is going to be 1/4th of the chest.

2 – 0 is the waist length.

3 – 0 is the full length.

4 – 0 is 1/12 of the chest.

5 – 0 is the same as 4 – 0.

X – 4= 5 – 0-2.5 cm [1 inch.]

Join X – 5 and shape the neck 5 – 4, as seen in the sketch draft.

6 – 0 = shoulder +1 cm [1/4".]

7 – 1= one fourth of the chest -1.5 cm. Join 6 and 7.

8 – 6= ¼ chest +4 – 5 cm [1/2"]

Join 4 – 8. 9 – 7= 3.25 cm [1 1/4"].

10 – 1= 1/4th of chest, +4 – 5 cm [1 ½ – 2"]

Shape the scye – 8 – 9 – 10.

Square down from 10 – 11.

12 – 11= 1.5 cm

13 – 3= 10 to 1+1.5 cm – ½ inch.

Shape the side seam 10 – 12 – 13

14 – 3 is equal to 2 cm [3/4"]

Shape the bottom – 14 – 13

15 – 14= 3.25 cm [1 ¼"]

16 – 1= 2.5 cm

Join 15 – 16.

17 – 4= 2 cm [3/4"]

Join the crease line 16 – 17

18 – 5= 4 cm – 1 ½" or according to your taste.

Shape the lapel 18 – 16

19 – 7= 1 inch [2.5".]

20 – 19= 1/8 of the chest, +1.5 cm [half an inch] for the pocket width.

Pocket height is width of the pocket +1.5 cm [half an inch.]

21 is midway between 12 – 2.

22 – 21 is about 1/12 of the chest.

22 is midway of the lower pocket, which is 1/8 of the chest, +2.5 – 4 cm or 1 – 1 ½ inches in width and the height is two centimeters ¼ inches more than the pocket width.

Back Drafting

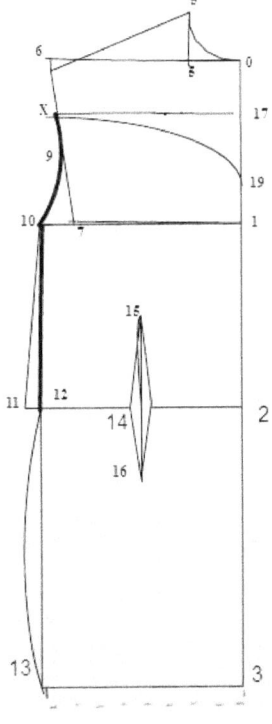

The fold is at 0 – 1 – 3.

Except for 5, 8, and 9 all the points from 0 – 30 are drawn in the same way as given in the front.

5 – 4= 2.5 cm. 8 – 6= 1.5 cm.

Join the shoulder. 5 – 8 and shape the scye 8 – 9 – 10 as shown in the draft.

14 is midway between 12 – 2.

15 – 14 and 16 – 14 is each about 1/6 of the chest.

Take half an inch dart at 14 if you want.

Collar

Square lines from 0, and fold that 0 – 1.

1 – 0 is 1/8 of the chest. 2 – 0 is half neck +1 cm.

3 – 1 is same as 2 – 0. Join 2 and 3.

4 – 3 is 3 – 4 cm according to your taste.

5 – 1 is half of 3 – 1. Center point of 3 – 1.

Shape 5 – 4. 6 – 2 is 1.5 cm. Join 4 – 6 and extend up to .7.

7 – 6= 3 – 4 cm [1 ¼ to 1 ½".]

Shape 7 – 0. Remember that an unfolded yoke has to be cut in the straight grain or in a bias, but not in a crosswise grain.

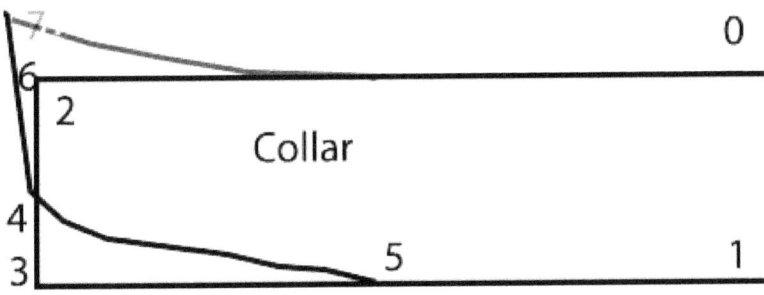

So now that we have finished practice drafts for men wear, the next volumes will have more about collars, sleeves, pants, and other garments, how to sew them, how to alter patterns and so on.

Author Bio

Dueep Jyot Singh is a Management and IT Professional who managed to gather Postgraduate qualifications in Management and English and Degrees in Science, French and Education while pursuing different enjoyable career options like being an hospital administrator, IT,SEO and HRD Database Manager/ trainer, movie , radio and TV scriptwriter, theatre artiste and public speaker, lecturer in French, Marketing and Advertising, ex-Editor of Hearts On Fire (now known as Solstice) Books Missouri USA, advice columnist and cartoonist, publisher and Aviation School trainer, ex-moderator on Medico.in, banker, student councilor ,travelogue writer … among other things!

One fine morning, she decided that she had enough of killing herself by Degrees and went back to her first love -- writing. It's more enjoyable! She already has 48 published academic and 14 fiction- in- different- genre books under her belt.

When she is not designing websites or making Graphic design illustrations for clients , she is browsing through old bookshops hunting for treasures, of which she has an enviable collection – including R.L. Stevenson, O.Henry, Dornford Yates, Maurice Walsh, De Maupassant, Victor Hugo, Sapper, C.N. Williamson, "Bartimeus" and the crown of her collection- Dickens "The Old Curiosity Shop," and "Martin Chuzzlewit" and so on… Just call her "Renaissance Woman" - collecting herbal remedies, acting like Universal Helping Hand/Agony Aunt, or escaping to her dear mountains for a bit of exploring, collecting herbs and plants, and trekking.

Check out some of the other JD-Biz Publishing books

Gardening Series on Amazon

Download Free Books!

http://MendonCottageBooks.com

Health Learning Series

THE MAGIC OF GOOSEBERRIES FOR HEALTH AND BEAUTY	THE MAGIC OF YOGURT FOR COOKING AND BEAUTY	THE MAGIC OF LEMONS USING LEMONS FOR HEALTH AND BEAUTY	THE MAGIC OF CHILLIES FOR COOKING AND HEALING	THE MAGIC OF ONIONS ONIONS IN CUISINE TO CURE AND TO HEAL	THE MAGIC OF RADISHES TO CURE AND TO HEAL
THE MAGIC OF CARROTS TO CURE AND TO HEAL	THE HEALTH BENEFITS OF OREGANO FOR COOKING AND HEALTH	The Magic Of MARIGOLDS Marigolds for Health And Beauty	THE HEALTH BENEFITS OF CINNAMON	THE MAGIC OF COCONUTS FOR COOKING & HEALTH	THE MAGIC OF CLOVES FOR HEALING AND COOKING
THE MAGIC OF ASAFETIDA FOR COOKING AND HEALING	THE MAGIC OF NEEM MARGOSA TO HEAL	THE MAGIC OF SALT TO HEAL AND FOR BEAUTY	THE MAGIC OF POMEGRANATES FOR HEALTH AND BEAUTY	THE MAGIC OF DRY FRUIT AND SPICES REMEDIES AND RECIPES	THE HEALTH BENEFITS OF TURMERIC CURCUMIN FOR COOKING AND HEALTH
THE MAGIC OF ALOE VERA	THE MAGIC OF VEGETABLES ANCIENT HEALING REMEDIES AND TIPS	THE HEALTH BENEFITS OF ROSEMARY FOR COOKING AND HEALTH	THE MAGIC OF PEPPER & PEPPERCORNS FOR COOKING & HEALING	THE MAGIC OF MILK, BUTTER AND CHEESE FOR COOKING & HEALING	THE MAGIC OF CARDAMOMS FOR COOKING AND HEALTH
THE HEALTH BENEFITS OF BLACK CUMIN FOR COOKING AND HEALTH	THE MAGIC OF BASIL-TULSI TO HEAL NATURALLY	THE MAGIC OF SPICES FOR HEALTH AND CUISINE	THE MAGIC OF ROSES FOR COOKING AND BEAUTY	The Miraculous Healing Powers of GINGER	The Miracle of HONEY

Country Life Books

Amazing Animal Book Series

Learn To Draw Series

How to Build and Plan Books

Entrepreneur Book Series

Our books are available at

1. Amazon.com

2. Barnes and Noble

3. Itunes

4. Kobo

5. Smashwords

6. Google Play Books

Download Free Books!

http://MendonCottageBooks.com

Publisher

JD-Biz Corp

P O Box 374

Mendon, Utah 84325

http://www.jd-biz.com/

Mendon Cottage Books

P O Box 374, Mendon Utah 84325

Mendon Cottage Books